The Heart of Leadership

Mastering Management in a Changing World

Gwendolyn Nadean Mathews

The Heart of Leadership

Mastering Management in a Changing World

Gwendolyn Nadean Mathews

Copyright © 2025 Gwendolyn Nadean Mathews

All rights reserved. This book or any portion thereof may not be reproduced or used in any manner whatsoever without the express written permission of the publisher except for the use of brief quotations in a book review.

First printing, 2026

Purple Peacock Press

PurplePeacockPress.com

ISBN: 978-1-960485-25-0 (paperback)

THE HEART OF LEADERSHIP

Mastering Management in a Changing World

GWENDOLYN MATHEWS

Contents

Preface	ix
Introduction	1
1. Leadership Styles	5
2. Ten Qualities of a Good Leader	21
3. Communication of a Good Leader	31
4. Culture and the Good Leader	41
5. Education in Leadership	49
6. Knowing When to Fold	57
7. A Look Into the Future of Leadership	67
8. The Golden Rule of Leadership	75
Author's Note: Why I Wrote This Book	81
About the Author	85

Preface
What I Hope to Achieve Through This Book

Writing The Heart of Leadership: Mastering Leadership in a Changing World has been a journey of reflection, purpose, and gratitude. After more than five decades of service in the field of Human Resources and leadership—rising through the ranks from entry-level to senior management—I felt a calling to share the lessons I've learned about people, leadership, and the strength it takes to lead with both firmness and compassion.

Over the years, I have encountered leaders of every kind: those who inspired others to reach higher, and those who led through fear or ego. Those experiences taught me that true leadership cannot exist without integrity, empathy, and accountability. Leadership is not about titles, authority, or control—it is about people. It's about guiding, listening, and lifting others as you climb.

My goal in writing this book is to help current and future leaders rediscover the human side of leadership. I want readers to see themselves in these pages—to reflect on their values, their leadership style, and their ability to adapt to change. I hope this book will serve as both a mirror and a map: a mirror to help readers reflect on who they are as leaders, and a map to guide them toward becoming the kind of leader who inspires growth, trust, and excellence in others.

If, after reading this book, even one person decides to lead with greater understanding, communicate more clearly, or show more compassion toward their team, then I will have achieved what I set out to do. Leadership begins and ends with the heart—and it is my sincere hope that the words within these pages will inspire others to lead from theirs.

With gratitude,

Gwendolyn Nadean Mathews

Author, The Heart of Leadership: Mastering Leadership in a Changing World

Dedication

This book is lovingly dedicated to my family—my children and my seven wonderful grandchildren—who are my greatest blessings and my daily inspiration. You have been my constant reminder that love, perseverance,

and faith are at the core of all true leadership.

To those who lead with compassion, integrity, and courage—

may these pages encourage you to keep leading from the heart

and to never lose sight of the people you serve.

With love and gratitude,

Gwendolyn Nadean Mathews

Introduction

LEADERSHIP IS EVOLVING in the twenty-first century. It's no longer just about authority or title—it's about influence, authenticity, and adaptability. With rapid technological advancement, shifting workforce demographics, and global interconnectivity, the need for thoughtful, resilient, and visionary leaders is greater than ever.

The world faces complex challenges: climate change, inequality, mental health crises, and more. Leadership in this environment requires more than charisma or command—it demands character, clarity.

Leadership and management are more than titles or positions—they are responsibilities, callings, and arts in themselves. Across industries and organizations—whether in the fast-paced world of startups, the structured hierarchy of the military, or the purpose-driven world of nonprofits—effective leadership and strong management are what differentiate thriving entities from stagnant ones.

Leadership is about vision. It's the spark that ignites change, the voice that rallies a team, and the compass that points toward the future. Great leaders inspire action, unlock potential, and navigate ambiguity with confidence. They lead people—not just projects or processes—with empathy, courage, and purpose.

Management, on the other hand, is about execution. It transforms the abstract into the actionable. A skilled manager brings order to chaos, optimizes performance, and ensures that the vision becomes a reality. Where leadership is often associated with the heart, management belongs to the hands and mind—organizing, coordinating, and problem-solving with precision.

Too often, leadership and management are presented as opposing forces. In reality, they are two sides of the same coin. Leadership without management leads to inspiration without results. Management without leadership produces efficiency without direction. The most effective professionals master both, learning when to inspire and when to structure, when to innovate and when to implement.

In this book, we explore what leadership truly means and how management supports or hinders it. We examine not only the traits of effective leaders but the decisions and behaviors that define them.

Example:

During the early days of the COVID-19 pandemic, New Zealand Prime Minister Jacinda Ardern demonstrated strong leadership by communicating with empathy and decisiveness, gaining global recognition for her clarity and compassion.

This book explores the full spectrum of leadership and management through theory, examples, and practical strategies. Each chapter delves into a vital element—from leadership styles and communication to culture, education, and knowing when to let go. You'll encounter lessons from historical figures, modern innovators, and real-world scenarios. The goal is not only to inform, but to transform—to help you grow into a leader who inspires and a manager who delivers.

Whether you're a seasoned executive, a team leader, an entrepreneur, or someone aspiring to lead in your own way, this book is designed for you. Leadership is not confined to the boardroom. It shows up in classrooms, communities, families, and friendships. If you're ready to grow, to reflect, and to lead with intention, you've come to the right place.

Let's begin the journey.

REFLECTION QUESTIONS

- How would you describe the difference between leadership and management in your own words?
- Can you recall a moment when someone truly led you—not managed you? What did they do that stood out?
- What aspects of leadership do you feel the strongest? Where do you want to grow?

QUOTE TO LEAD BY

"The function of leadership is to produce more leaders, not more followers." – Ralph Nader

Chapter One

Leadership Styles

The Power of Style in Leadership

There is no one-size-fits all when it comes to leadership. Just as no two people are exactly the same, no two leaders lead exactly alike. The most effective leaders understand this. They don't force a style—they adapt to the moment, to the team, and to the outcome they're working toward.

Leadership styles are essentially the approaches or behaviors leaders use to influence, motivate, and guide others. Your leadership style not only affects how your team performs, but also how they feel, how they grow, and how loyal they are to your vision.

Leadership styles are not rigid categories—they are tools. The most effective leaders are those who understand their own natural tendencies while remaining agile enough to adapt their style to the moment. Whether you're rallying a team through change, building from scratch, or managing stability, your approach to leadership can shape outcomes far beyond your intentions.

In this chapter, we break down the core leadership styles—how they work, when they shine, and what pitfalls to avoid. You may find your own reflection in one or more of them. The goal is not to pick one—it's to grow into all of them as needed.

Autocratic Leadership: Command and Control

> "A good leader takes a little more than his share of the blame, a little less than his share of the credit."
>
> — *Arnold H. Glasow*

Autocratic leadership centralizes power and decision-making in the hands of one person. This style is characterized by strict control, minimal input from subordinates, and an expectation of unquestioned compliance. While it can lead to efficiency in crisis situations, it often suppresses creativity and discourages employee engagement.

Example:

Martha Stewart built a billion-dollar empire with a precise vision and firm control. Similarly, at Rollins Electric Company, CEO Mr. Johnson calls his senior leaders into meetings to discuss ways to increase profits. Though he considers himself democratic, his leadership is autocratic—ego-driven, dismissive of feedback, and intolerant of dissent. Employees quickly learn that questioning him may cost them their jobs.

Reflection Questions:

1. Have you ever worked under an autocratic leader? How did it impact your motivation and performance?
2. When might an autocratic approach be necessary in leadership?
3. How can leaders maintain authority without silencing innovation or morale?

Autocratic leadership is direct and decisive. Leaders make decisions swiftly, set clear expectations, and expect adherence. This approach thrives in environments where speed, structure, and precision are paramount—think emergency response, military strategy, or high-stakes turnarounds.

Strengths: Fast decision-making, clear roles, tight control.

Risks: Can suppress innovation and demoralize teams if overused.

Use this style sparingly, and only when urgency trumps collaboration. When the storm passes, so should the command-and-control mindset.

Democratic Leadership: Leading Through Consensus

Leadership and learning are indispensable to each other."

— *John F. Kennedy*

Democratic leaders balance authority with participation. They invite feedback, encourage collaboration, and value the collective wisdom of their team. This approach fosters trust, engagement, and accountability while maintaining clear leadership direction.

Example:

As an HR leader, Joan McIntosh faced a daunting challenge—processing 2,500 personnel actions each day. Instead of dictating orders, she convened her team to brainstorm solutions. Through open discussion and shared ownership, the group devised new methods and embraced the process. Joan made the final decisions, but her team felt heard, valued, and motivated.

Notable Democratic Leaders:

Barack Obama • Nelson Mandela • John F. Kennedy • Mahatma Gandhi • Martin Luther King Jr.

Reflection Questions:

1. How can involving others in decision-making improve outcomes in your workplace?
2. What are the risks of being "too democratic" as a leader?
3. How can you encourage open dialogue while staying decisive?
4. Democratic leaders foster dialogue, encourage team input, and build collective ownership over decisions. It creates a collaborative culture where

diverse perspectives inform smarter, more inclusive outcomes.

Strengths: High engagement, better decision-making, stronger team cohesion.

Risks: Slower processes, risk of indecision when consensus is elusive.

Use this style when creativity, buy-in, and shared ownership are essential. Just remember—democracy doesn't mean indecision. The leader still leads.

Transformational Leadership: Inspiring Vision

> "People buy into the leader before they buy into the vision."
>
> — John C. Maxwell

Transformational leaders inspire others to dream bigger, work harder, and achieve more. They possess charisma, vision, and a deep belief in the potential of their people. This style promotes loyalty, personal growth, and innovation.

Example:

Walmart founder Sam Walton embodied transformational leadership. He regularly visited stores, spoke with employees, and celebrated their contributions. His belief in appreciation and inclusion created a culture where people took pride in their work—and in turn, fueled Walmart's rise as a global leader.

Notable Transformational Leaders:

Oprah Winfrey • Franklin D. Roosevelt • Angela Merkel

Reflection Questions:

1. Who has inspired you to become a better version of yourself, and how?
2. How can you motivate your team beyond monetary rewards?
3. What personal traits make a leader truly transformational?

Transformational leaders lead with passion, vision, and a deep sense of purpose. They challenge teams to go beyond what's expected, often pushing boundaries and redefining what's possible.

Strengths: Drives innovation, builds loyalty, elevates performance.

Risks: Vision without action can feel hollow; burnout is a danger.

This style works best when you're leading change, launching new initiatives, or seeking long-term cultural shifts. Fuel inspiration with execution.

Transactional Leadership: Structure and Rewards

"The best way to predict your future is to create it."

— *Peter Drucker*

Transactional leadership emphasizes structure, rules, and performance-based rewards. It thrives in environments where tasks are measurable and accountability is critical. Success is built on order, discipline, and results.

Example:

When Joan McIntosh needed to complete 2,500 personnel actions within one week, she temporarily shifted from democratic to transactional leadership. She implemented metrics and incentives—rewarding top performers and addressing underperformance directly. The system clarified expectations, drove productivity, and met the organization's goals.

Notable Transactional Leaders:

General Norman Schwarzkopf Jr. • Bill Gates • Vince Lombardi

Reflection Questions:

1. How can rewards and recognition improve employee performance?
2. What are the potential downsides of relying too heavily on rules and rewards?
3. When might a transactional approach be more effective than a transformational one?

Transactional leadership is built on structure, performance standards, and a clear system of rewards and consequences. It works best in environments where consistency, efficiency, and order are priorities.

Strengths: Clear accountability, predictable outcomes, solid for routine tasks.

Risks: Can feel impersonal or mechanical; doesn't inspire growth or innovation.

This is a solid foundation for large teams or regulated environments. Just don't mistake compliance for commitment.

Servant Leadership: Putting People First

"The first responsibility of a leader is to define reality. The last is to say thank you. In between, the leader is a servant."

— *Max DePree*

Servant leaders prioritize service above status. They focus on the well-being and growth of others, believing that empowered teams drive lasting success. This style requires humility, empathy, and moral courage.

Examples:

Abraham Lincoln: *Demonstrated compassion and equality by leading America through its darkest hours and abolishing slavery.*

Mother Teresa: *Devoted her life to serving the poor, sick, and forgotten, with no desire for personal gain.*

The Dalai Lama: *Leads with peace and empathy, promoting compassion across religious and cultural divides.*

Herb Kelleher (Southwest Airlines): *Believed that "the business of business is people," fostering a culture of care and respect.*

Cheryl Bachelder (Popeyes): *Credited her company's success to servant leadership principles—putting others first and leading by example.*

Reflection Questions:

1. How does servant leadership build trust within an organization?
2. What sacrifices might be necessary to lead with a servant's heart?

3. How can humility coexist with authority in leadership?

Servant leaders flip the traditional model—placing the needs of others at the center. They build trust, support development, and create space for others to thrive.

Strengths: Builds trust, strong relationships, high team morale.

Risks: May lack direction or control if not balanced with assertiveness.

In people-driven fields, this style builds loyalty and psychological safety. Combine it with vision and strategy, and you have a leader others want to follow.

Laissez-Faire Leadership: Freedom and Flexibility

> "As we look ahead into the next century, leaders will be those who empower others."
>
> — *Bill Gates*

Laissez-faire leadership allows teams the autonomy to make decisions and manage their work with minimal interference. It fosters creativity and ownership but requires mature, self-motivated employees to succeed.

Example:

An Executive Officer tasked their team with developing a new salary scale for the organization, offering limited direction but full trust. This approach empowered employees to collaborate, innovate, and take ownership—building confidence and accountability in the process.

Reflection Questions:

1. When is it appropriate for leaders to step back and allow others to lead?
2. How can trust be maintained without constant oversight?
3. What skills must employees have to thrive under a laissez-faire leader?

Laissez-faire leaders trust their teams to make decisions and manage their work. It's a hands-off approach that fosters autonomy and ownership—when used in the right context.

Strengths: Encourages independence, supports innovation.

Risks: Can lead to confusion, lack of alignment, or low productivity.

Use this style with high-performing, self-directed individuals. Provide direction upfront, then step back and let them excel.

Situational Leadership: Adaptive Excellence

Situational leadership is the art of flexing. Developed by Paul Hersey and Ken Blanchard, it emphasizes reading the context and adapting your approach based on the needs, skill levels, and motivations of your team.

Strengths: Highly flexible, context-aware, empowering.

Risks: Requires strong emotional intelligence and self-awareness.

This style is the gold standard in modern leadership: tailored, thoughtful, and responsive. It's not about abandoning principles—it's about delivering them in the right way at the right time.

Closing Reflection: What's Your Style?

Leadership styles are not labels—they're tools. Knowing your primary style is helpful, but growth comes from learning to stretch. Ask yourself:

- Where am I most comfortable as a leader?
- What style does my team need more of right now?
- Which style challenges me the most—and why?

Leadership Style Self-Assessment & Reflection

Step 1: *Quick Self-Check — What's Your Natural Style?*

Read the following statements and mark the ones that resonate most with you. Then tally your results to get a sense of your dominant leadership style.

Instructions: Check all that apply under each style. You may check statements across multiple styles.

Autocratic Leader

☐ I prefer to make decisions quickly and expect others to follow.

☐ I value efficiency and control in fast-moving situations.

☐ I believe structure and discipline drive performance.

Democratic Leader

☐ I regularly ask my team for their ideas before making decisions.

☐ I believe collaboration leads to better solutions.

☐ I aim to build consensus and buy-in before moving forward.

Transformational Leader

☐ I enjoy inspiring others with vision and big-picture goals.

☐ I want to challenge people to be their best selves.

☐ I focus on long-term change and continuous improvement.

Transactional Leader

☐ I like clear expectations and measurable goals.

☐ I use rewards and consequences to shape behavior.

☐ I believe structure and order are essential for success.

Servant Leader

☐ I put the needs of others before my own as a leader.

☐ I believe in supporting and empowering my team.

☐ I lead by listening and creating safe environments for growth.

Laissez-Faire Leader

☐ I trust my team to manage their work without much interference.

☐ I believe in giving people freedom to figure things out.

☐ I prefer a flexible, hands-off approach.

Situational Leader

☐ I adjust my approach depending on who I'm leading and the situation.

☐ I often change styles based on the context.

☐ I believe flexibility is more important than consistency in leadership style.

Step 2: *Tally and Reflect*

- Which styles had the most checkmarks?
- Which had the least?
- Are you surprised by your results?

Your dominant style(s):

_____

Your most underused style(s):

_____

Step 3: Leadership Style Reflection Questions

Take a few minutes to journal or think through the following:

1. Which leadership style do you naturally lean toward, and why?
2. Think about a time when your natural style worked really well. What was the situation?
3. Now think about a time it didn't. What might you have done differently?
4. Which style do you want to strengthen? What's one way you could practice that in the next 30 days?
5. How does your leadership style align (or clash) with the needs of your current team?

WORKBOOK EXERCISES

1. What are your key takeaways from this chapter?

2. How can you apply one lesson from this chapter in your leadership journey this week?

3. What's one commitment you'll make based on what you've learned?

Use the space below to journal your responses:

Chapter Two

Ten Qualities of a Good Leader

A DEPARTMENT HEAD of a large manufacturing firm faced uncertainty and anxiety during a major restructuring project. Employees resisted change out of fear—fear of job loss, new workloads, and an unfamiliar structure.

As the leader, she knew her responsibility was to communicate the changes clearly and address every concern with honesty and empathy. In a team meeting, she explained the purpose of the restructuring and reassured employees that their roles were secure. She listened to their feedback, acknowledged their fears, and emphasized the opportunities

By creating a space where employees felt valued, safe, and motivated, she transformed anxiety into trust. Her open communication and decisive leadership enabled the restructuring project to be completed smoothly and successfully—without a single disruption.

One: Vision

A good leader begins with vision. Vision isn't just about seeing the future—it's about shaping it. Leaders with vision are able to see beyond the current circumstances and anticipate trends, challenges, and opportunities. They imagine what is possible, then inspire others to believe in that possibility. Vision provides direction, motivation, and purpose. It sets the tone for the team or organization.

Visionary leaders don't just react to change—they drive it. Whether it's Martin Luther King Jr.'s dream for civil rights, Sam Walton, Wal-Mart Founder, or Reed Hastings, CEO of Netflix, the best leaders articulate a compelling vision that becomes a guiding star for everyone they lead.

Two: Integrity

Integrity is the bedrock of trust, and trust is the currency of leadership. A leader's ability to inspire, influence, and guide others depends largely on the belief that they are honest, ethical, and reliable. Without integrity, everything else collapses.

Leaders with integrity are consistent in their actions, words, and decisions. They don't play favorites or shift their values for convenience. They do the right thing—even when it's hard, even when no one is watching. This moral compass creates psychological safety for their teams, fosters loyalty, and sets a standard that others follow.

Integrity isn't perfection. It's about accountability, transparency, and the courage to admit mistakes. Leaders who own their failures demonstrate strength, not weakness.

Three: Emotional Intelligence (EI)

Great leaders don't just lead projects—they lead people. And people are emotional creatures. Emotional intelligence —the ability to recognize, understand, manage, and influence emotions—is a crucial quality for effective leadership.

Leaders with high EQ are self-aware and self-regulating. They know their triggers, control their impulses, and approach problems with empathy. They read the room. They pick up on non-verbal cues, sense when a team member is struggling, and create space for authentic conversation. They give feedback without crushing confidence and offer praise without creating complacency.

In environments led by emotionally intelligent leaders, there is less drama, more collaboration, and a stronger sense of belonging.

Four: Decisiveness

Leadership demands decisions—sometimes hard, high-stakes, and time-sensitive ones. A good leader gathers input, evaluates options, and acts. Indecision breeds confusion, stalls momentum, and weakens credibility.

Decisiveness doesn't mean recklessness. It means having the courage to choose a path, the wisdom to change direction if needed, and the humility to learn from the outcome. People trust leaders who can make decisions and stand by them, even in uncertainty.

The best leaders are also transparent about their decision-making process. They explain their reasoning, acknowledge trade-offs, and involve others when appropriate. This approach not only strengthens decisions but also earns respect and buy-in.

Five: Adaptability

In a rapidly changing world, rigidity is a liability. Adaptability is the ability to pivot, innovate, and stay relevant. Good leaders are flexible without being fickle. They adjust strategies while holding on to their core values and vision.

Adaptable leaders embrace change as an opportunity, not a threat. They don't panic when things deviate from the plan—instead, they stay curious, seek input, and experiment. They empower teams to try new things, fail fast, and grow smarter.

Leadership isn't about having all the answers. It's about navigating complexity with grace, helping others do the same, and constantly.

Six: Communication Skills

Sarah, the leader of a major technology organization, noticed that a high-performing employee, Francie, had recently begun underperforming—missing deadlines, skipping meetings, and showing signs of disengagement.

Instead of ignoring the issue, Sarah scheduled a private meeting to understand the underlying problem. Through a compassionate and structured conversation, she learned that Francie had taken on caregiving responsibilities for her ill parents and was feeling overwhelmed but fearful of losing her job.

Sarah set the tone of understanding and collaboration. She presented examples of missed expectations, listened to Francie's challenges, and worked with her to develop a solution. Together, they agreed on adjustments, including connecting Francie with the Employee Assistance Program for caregiver support.

Within months, Francie regained her balance and returned to being a top performer. This experience demonstrated the power of communication rooted in empathy, clarity, and accountability.

Leadership is as much about what you say as how you say it. Clear, confident, and compassionate communication fosters understanding, alignment, and trust. Great leaders articulate vision, set expectations, give feedback, and listen—really listen.

Strong communication also involves storytelling. Great leaders know how to use stories to inspire, humanize their message, and build emotional connection. They understand tone, timing, and audience.

Importantly, they don't dominate conversations—they facilitate them. They create forums for open dialogue, encourage diverse perspectives, and respond, not react.

Seven: Accountability

Leaders set the tone for responsibility. When leaders hold themselves accountable, it cascades through the organization. They take accountability for outcomes—good and bad. They don't blame, deflect, or hide. They reflect, learn, and act.

Accountability is not about punishment. It's about commitment to standards and the willingness to be answerable for results. Leaders who embrace accountability empower others to do the same.

They also create systems where accountability is mutual. Everyone—from interns to executives—is responsible for contributing, speaking up, and improving. This builds a culture of trust and performance.

Eight: Servant Mindset

At its core, leadership is service. It's not about titles or control—it's about elevating others. Great leaders flip the pyramid. They ask, "How can I help my team succeed?" instead of "How can they help me look good?"

Servant leaders are humble, approachable, and generous with their time. They remove obstacles, provide resources, and advocate for their people. They measure success not by personal gain, but by collective growth.

This mindset creates loyalty, engagement, and psychological safety. When people feel seen, heard, and supported, they bring their full selves to the table.

Nine: Courage

Leadership often requires walking alone, making unpopular decisions, and taking risks. Courage is the backbone that allows leaders to do what's right—not just what's easy. It fuels change, innovation, and justice.

Courageous leaders speak truth to power, challenge the status quo, and stand up for their teams. They don't shy away from conflict or discomfort. Instead, they lean in, guided by principle.

They also cultivate courage in others. By modeling bravery, they empower others to take initiative, share bold ideas, and speak up—even when it's scary.

Ten: Consistency

In leadership, consistency builds trust. Teams thrive when they know what to expect from their leader—emotionally, ethically, and operationally. Consistent leaders are predictable in the best sense: stable, fair, and dependable.

Consistency in vision, messaging, behavior, and standards ensures alignment. It prevents chaos and helps teams focus. When leaders show up consistently, others feel safe to do the same.

Consistency doesn't mean rigidity. It means having a steady hand on the wheel—even when the seas get rough.

Reflections

Reflecting on the qualities of a good leader, one truth becomes clear: leadership is not about being the smartest person in the room—it's about empowering others to be their best selves. The most effective leaders blend strength with empathy, vision with humility, and decisiveness with openness.

No leader is perfect. But what separates great leaders is their commitment to growth. They are constantly learning—about themselves, their teams, and the world around them. They seek feedback, adapt, and evolve. Leadership isn't a destination; it's a journey.

As you reflect on your own leadership path, ask yourself:

- Which qualities do I already embody?
- Which ones challenge me?
- What would it look like to lead with greater integrity, empathy, or courage?

Growth begins with awareness—and leadership grows from the inside out.

Quotes

> "The greatest leader is not necessarily the one who does the greatest things. He is the one that gets the people to do the greatest things." — Ronald Reagan

---

> "Before you are a leader, success is all about growing yourself. When you become a leader, success is all about growing others."— Jack Welch

---

> "Leadership is not about being in charge. It is about taking care of those in your charge." — Simon Sinek

"Courage is the first virtue that makes all other virtues possible." — Aristotle

---

"People don't care how much you know until they know how much you care." — Theodore Roosevelt

---

"You manage things; you lead people." — Rear Admiral Grace Hopper

---

"To handle yourself, use your head; to handle others, use your heart." — Eleanor Roosevelt

---

"In the end, it is important to remember that we cannot become what we need to be by remaining what we are."

— Max De Pree

Chapter Three
Communication of a Good Leader

Mr. Cooper led one of the most successful teams at Brightview Nursing Center. While most employees were committed to delivering high-quality patient care, a few displayed disengagements and failed to meet the standards expected of the team.

Understanding that effective communication is essential to maintaining both performance and morale, Mr. Cooper called a meeting. He communicated the Nursing Center's mission and goals with clarity and purpose, reinforcing what excellence looked like and why it mattered. He acknowledged the team's overall success while honestly addressing that some behaviors were not aligned with the organization's expectations.

Mr. Cooper paid close attention to nonverbal cues during the meeting and addressed them directly. He clearly stated that disengaged behavior would not be tolerated and that accountability would follow if expectations were not met. At the same time, he communicated respect by inviting anyone who felt unable to meet the standards to speak with him privately rather than calling out individuals publicly.

By communicating expectations clearly, listening attentively, and addressing issues with firmness and respect, Mr. Cooper reinforced trust and accountability. When those employees met with him afterward, they expressed appreciation for his honesty and transparency and committed to improving their performance to align with the team's values and commitment to exceptional patient care.

The Power of Communication in Leadership

Communication is one of the most vital and foundational skills a leader can possess. It is the bridge between vision and execution, intention and understanding, strategy and action. Without effective communication, even the most brilliant ideas can be misunderstood or lost altogether. Good communication aligns teams, motivates individuals, resolves conflicts, and creates cultures of transparency and trust.

A leader's communication style has the power to either inspire or alienate, clarify or confuse, unite or divide. For this reason, communication must be intentional, authentic, and adaptive. Let's explore the dimensions and dynamics of effective communication in leadership.

Clarity and Precision

Great leaders communicate clearly and precisely. They avoid jargon and ambiguity, ensuring that their messages are easily understood. Clarity helps reduce confusion, sets accurate expectations, and enables teams to execute efficiently. When leaders speak clearly, they create alignment and confidence.

Clear communication also reflects clear thinking. Leaders must take time to organize their thoughts and tailor their language to their audience. Whether outlining a strategic plan or giving daily instructions, clarity should always be a priority.

Active Listening

Communication is a two-way process. Listening—especially active listening—is a critical skill for any leader. Active listening involves being fully present, withholding judgment, and seeking to understand before responding. It means tuning in not just to words, but to tone, emotion, and body language.

When leaders listen well, they build trust and rapport. They demonstrate respect and empathy, which strengthens relationships. Listening also provides valuable insights that help leaders make better decisions and detect potential problems early.

Great leaders ask open-ended questions, paraphrase for understanding, and create space for others to express themselves honestly. They know that listening is not a passive act—it's a powerful form of engagement.

Nonverbal Communication

A leader's message doesn't just come through their words. It's also conveyed through body language, facial expressions, tone of voice, and eye contact. These nonverbal cues can either reinforce or undermine what is being said.

For instance, a leader may say they are open to feedback, but if their arms are crossed and they avoid eye contact, the message may not feel genuine. Leaders must be aware of their nonverbal signals and ensure they align with their words.

Nonverbal communication also helps leaders convey confidence, empathy, and openness. A calm and confident demeanor in times of crisis can reassure a team even more than words can.

Storytelling

Storytelling is one of the most powerful tools a leader can use. Stories captivate attention, evoke emotion, and make abstract concepts relatable. They help people remember information and connect with the values and purpose behind a leader's message.

Leaders use stories to share lessons, reinforce culture, celebrate success, and communicate vision. A compelling story can transform a routine announcement into a memorable moment. It can turn a strategic goal into a shared mission.

Good leaders don't just tell stories—they invite others into the story. They make team members feel like co-authors of the journey.

Transparency and Honesty

Trust is built on transparency and honesty. Leaders who communicate openly—about challenges, changes, successes, and failures—create environments where people feel respected and included.

Transparency doesn't mean oversharing or causing unnecessary alarm. It means providing the right level of information at the right time, being clear about what is known and unknown, and being honest when things go wrong.

Honest communication fosters credibility. When leaders tell the truth, even when it's hard, they earn the loyalty and respect of their teams.

Adaptability in Communication Style

Different situations—and different people—require different communication approaches. A great leader is adaptable. They know when to be direct and when to be diplomatic. They understand that some individuals prefer details while others respond better to big-picture thinking.

Cultural background, personality type, and context all influence how people receive messages. Leaders who adapt their style while staying authentic are more likely to connect with diverse audiences and inspire action.

Adapting doesn't mean changing your core message—it means delivering it in a way that resonates.

Giving and Receiving Feedback

Feedback is one of the most powerful tools for growth. Great leaders not only provide constructive feedback—they also invite and receive it. Feedback, when done well, improves performance, strengthens relationships, and fosters a culture of continuous improvement.

Effective feedback is timely, specific, and focused on behaviors rather than personal traits. It is delivered with empathy and the intention to help the recipient grow. Leaders also make feedback a two-way street, creating safe spaces for team members to share their own perspectives.

Receiving feedback with humility shows that a leader is still learning—and that they value their team's insights.

Crisis Communication

In times of crisis, communication becomes even more critical. People look to leaders for clarity, stability, and direction. A calm and composed tone, paired with factual information and empathy, helps teams stay grounded.

Great leaders communicate frequently during a crisis. They update their teams as new information becomes available, acknowledge fears and uncertainties, and share the steps being taken to address the situation.

Consistency and presence are vital. Leaders who show up and communicate regularly during turbulent times build trust and resilience.

Vision Communication

Leaders are custodians of vision. It's not enough to have a vision; leaders must communicate it with passion and clarity. A well-communicated vision inspires, energizes, and provides meaning. It helps teams understand not just what they are doing—but why.

The most compelling visions are communicated through a mix of logic and emotion. Leaders paint a vivid picture of the future while linking it to shared values and goals. They repeat the vision often and integrate it into daily conversations and decisions.

Vision communication turns ideas into movements.

Empowering Through Communication

Finally, great leaders use communication to empower others. They encourage initiative, validate contributions, and ensure everyone feels heard. Empowering communication is inclusive, affirming, and action-oriented.

When leaders communicate in ways that affirm people's strengths and potential, they ignite self-belief. When they invite collaboration and diverse viewpoints, they unlock innovation.

Empowering communication turns followers into leaders. It fosters ownership, pride, and purpose across the team.

Reflections

Communication is the soul of leadership. It is how leaders express who they are, what they value, and where they're going. Every conversation, email, gesture, and story contributes to the leadership message.

No leader communicates perfectly. But every leader can communicate with more intention, clarity, and heart. As you reflect on your own leadership communication, consider:

- Do I listen as well as I speak?
- Do my words match my actions?
- Do I create space for others to speak and feel heard?

Great communication starts with self-awareness and a deep respect for the people you lead. It is not just about transmitting information—it's about transforming understanding.

Quotes

"The art of communication is the language of leadership." — James Humes

---

"Wise men speak because they have something to say; fools because they have to say something." — Plato

---

"The most important thing in communication is hearing what isn't said." — Peter Drucker

"Leadership is about making others better as a result of your presence—and making sure that impact lasts in your absence." — Sheryl Sandberg

"Speak clearly, if you speak at all; carve every word before you let it fall." — Oliver Wendell Holmes

"To effectively communicate, we must realize that we are all different in the way we perceive the world." — Tony Robbins

"Listening is an art that requires attention over talent, spirit over ego, others over self." — Dean Jackson

Chapter Four
Culture and the Good Leader

The Importance of Culture in Leadership

IN SEVERAL OF my leadership roles within the elite organization where I managed, one of my first priorities upon assuming a new assignment was to meet the staff as a group before holding individual meetings. During this initial session, I clearly communicated my values, expectations, and how they aligned with the organization's mission and core principles. I emphasized that every team member played an important role in our collective success and encouraged inclusion, collaboration, and respect for diverse perspectives.

I assured the team that open communication was welcomed and that they could take risks without fear of blame if an initiative did not succeed. Accountability was important, but so was learning from our experiences. My goal was to foster an environment where employees felt connected to the organization's purpose and empowered to grow as both individuals and as part of the team.

In one particular instance, I supervised an employee who was assigned to a special project. Although this individual demonstrated potential, they struggled with attendance. When they later requested overtime to make up for missed time, I had to deny the request. I explained that granting overtime under those circumstances would send the wrong message to other employees—those who consistently showed up and carried their share of the workload. Allowing one person to compensate for poor attendance through overtime would not only seem unfair, but could also negatively affect morale.

As a leader, it was important to model fairness and consistency, reinforcing that responsibility and reliability are essential components of a positive workplace culture. True leadership means addressing issues directly and using them as teaching moments that strengthen both the individual and the team.

Culture is the invisible force that shapes behavior, influences decisions, and drives performance within any organization. For leaders, understanding and cultivating a positive, intentional culture is as vital as setting goals or managing resources. Culture is not a byproduct of leadership—it is a reflection of it.

A good leader doesn't just respond to culture—they actively shape it. Through their values, behaviors, language, and decisions, leaders model the culture they want to see. They understand that culture is the heartbeat of a team or organization: if it's strong and healthy, everything else can flourish. If it's toxic or neglected, even the best strategies will struggle to succeed.

Let's explore the components of a healthy culture and the role of leadership in building and sustaining it.

Defining and Living Core Values

Every strong culture starts with clear, shared values. These values act as a compass for behavior and decision-making. Good leaders define these values explicitly, but more importantly, they live them consistently. It's not enough to have words on a wall; values must be visible in everyday actions.

When leaders embody core values like respect, accountability, collaboration, and innovation, they give those values credibility. When they celebrate others who live those values, they reinforce cultural norms. A culture built on lived values becomes self-reinforcing and scalable.

Modeling Behavior

Leaders set the tone for what is acceptable, celebrated, and condemned within a culture. People pay more attention to what leaders do than what they say. A leader who promotes open communication but shuts down dissent sends a confusing signal. A leader who preaches work-life balance but glorifies overwork undermines the culture they're trying to build.

Modeling positive behavior means demonstrating humility, ownership, empathy, and fairness. It means showing up with consistency and integrity. Culture doesn't grow from mandates—it grows from modeling.

Creating Psychological Safety

Psychological safety—the belief that one can speak up, take risks, and admit mistakes without fear of punishment—is a critical element of a healthy culture. Good leaders create this safety through their own vulnerability and responsiveness.

When team members feel safe, they are more creative, engaged, and resilient. They collaborate better, raise concerns sooner, and take ownership more freely. Cultures with high psychological safety outperform those driven by fear and control.

Leaders build safety by listening actively, thanking people for their honesty, encouraging learning from failure, and rewarding courage over comfort.

Encouraging Diversity and Inclusion

Culture thrives on diversity. Different backgrounds, perspectives, and ideas fuel innovation and create a richer, more adaptive organization. But diversity without inclusion is incomplete. Inclusion is what ensures everyone feels valued and empowered to contribute.

Good leaders prioritize both. They recruit diverse talent, address bias, and create spaces where all voices can be heard. They challenge their own assumptions and facilitate equity in decision-making.

A culture of inclusion doesn't happen by accident—it happens through intentional leadership.

Communication as a Cultural Tool

Culture lives and breathes through communication. The way leaders talk about people, projects, and problems signals what's important. Transparent, consistent, and compassionate communication fosters trust and alignment.

Leaders use stories to reinforce cultural values. They share examples of team members living the culture. They talk openly about challenges and how cultural principles guide their responses. They use language intentionally to inspire, unite, and build identity.

Culture-building leaders don't just communicate from the top—they create open channels for dialogue across the organization.

Celebrating Wins and Learning from Losses

Culture is shaped not only by how success is achieved but by how it is recognized. Leaders build strong cultures by celebrating both outcomes and behaviors. Recognizing individuals who live the company values reinforces what matters.

Equally, good leaders shape culture by how they handle setbacks. They don't assign blame or avoid responsibility. Instead, they frame mistakes as learning opportunities and model resilience. This approach creates a culture of continuous improvement and humility.

Rituals, Traditions, and Symbols

Every organization has rituals and symbols that reinforce its culture—whether it's weekly team huddles, annual retreats, or shared language. Leaders who recognize the power of these cultural markers use them to strengthen unity and identity.

These traditions become part of what makes a workplace meaningful. They connect people to each other and to the organization's purpose. Good leaders build and protect these rituals, ensuring they evolve as the team grows.

Symbols—like badges, mission statements, or internal awards—also play a role in culture. When thoughtfully designed, they remind people of who they are and what they stand for.

Culture as a Strategic Asset

Leaders who invest in culture understand that it's not just a "nice to have"—it's a competitive advantage. Culture affects recruitment, retention, innovation, productivity, and reputation. In a world where talent is mobile and expectations are high; a strong culture attracts and retains the best.

When culture is aligned with strategy, performance follows. People don't just comply—they commit. They don't just execute—they innovate. Culture turns teams into movements and organizations into communities.

A good leader treats culture with the same urgency and rigor as any financial or operational priority.

Reflections

Culture is often invisible until it's broken. But great leaders see it clearly—and nurture it deliberately. They know that culture is not created by slogans or posters, but by people. Every conversation, decision, and ritual shapes it.

As a leader, ask yourself:

- What behaviors are encouraged or tolerated on my team?
- Do my actions reflect the culture I want to build?
- Are our values real or just rhetorical?

Culture isn't static. It evolves with each new hire, each new challenge, each new moment of truth. The question is: will that evolution be intentional—or accidental?

Good leaders answer that question with purpose.

Quotes

"Culture eats strategy for breakfast." — Peter Drucker

"You can have all the right strategy in the world; if you don't have the right culture, you're dead." — Patrick Whitesell

---

"The way to develop the best that is in a person is by appreciation and encouragement." — Charles Schwab

"If you don't manage your culture, it will manage you." — Edgar Schein

---

"What you do has far greater impact than what you say." — Stephen R. Covey

---

"The culture of any organization is shaped by the worst behavior the leader is willing to tolerate." — Gruenter and Whitaker

---

"Strong cultures help good people do great work." — Unknown

"In the long run, the most important single factor in success is a strong and vibrant corporate culture." — James L. Heskett

Chapter Five
Education in Leadership

DURING MY CAREER at an elite government agency, I was given the privilege of organizing a three-day Human Resources conference. I gathered my team, discussed plans and priorities, and—most importantly—listened to their feedback. Together, we produced one of the most successful HR conferences the agency had ever held.

In previous years, leaders of this event received monetary awards. Under new HR leadership, however, I was instead rewarded in a different way: the agency sponsored my Master's Degree in Personnel and Human Resources from American University in Washington, D.C.

That educational investment profoundly shaped my professional journey. Education cultivates critical thinking, problem-solving, and adaptability—skills that allow leaders to navigate complexity and lead with confidence. It reminds us that learning is not confined to the classroom but continues throughout our careers.

The Role of Education in Leadership

Education is a foundational pillar of effective leadership. While some leadership qualities may be innate—such as charisma or resilience—many others are developed through learning, reflection, and experience. Education equips leaders with the tools to think critically, communicate effectively, make informed decisions, and lead with vision and purpose.

Leadership education is not confined to formal degrees or structured programs. It encompasses continuous learning through experience, mentorship, books, workshops, feedback, and self-assessment. Great leaders are lifelong learners—they seek out knowledge, reflect on their actions, and are open to new perspectives.

Foundational Knowledge

At its core, leadership education provides foundational knowledge in areas such as management, communication, organizational behavior, ethics, psychology, and strategy. Understanding these disciplines helps leaders grasp the complex dynamics of teams and organizations.

For example, studying communication theory can improve how a leader delivers messages. Learning about psychology can help in motivating teams. Courses in ethics help leaders navigate dilemmas with integrity. This broad base of knowledge supports more effective and responsible leadership.

Critical Thinking and Decision-Making

Education sharpens critical thinking—an essential trait for leaders who face complex challenges and must evaluate competing priorities. A well-educated leader is better able to analyze information, consider multiple viewpoints, and make decisions grounded in logic, empathy, and ethics.

Leadership is rarely about choosing between right and wrong; more often, it involves navigating between competing goods or lesser evils. Educational experiences, such as case studies and debates, provide a safe environment to practice these decision-making skills.

Emotional Intelligence Development

Formal and informal educational settings help leaders develop emotional intelligence. Training programs focused on self-awareness, emotional regulation, empathy, and social skills enable leaders to build stronger relationships and manage conflict more effectively.

Emotional intelligence can be cultivated through reflection exercises, role-playing, group discussions, and feedback mechanisms—all of which are common in leadership development programs.

Learning from History and Role Models

Studying the lives and actions of historical leaders offers valuable lessons. History is filled with examples of leadership excellence and failure. Analyzing these stories helps aspiring leaders understand what works, what doesn't, and why.

Leaders can also learn from contemporary role models. Mentorship programs and biographies provide insight into real-world applications of leadership principles. Observing how respected leaders handle adversity, communicate, and inspire others can accelerate growth.

Cultivating a Growth Mindset

Leadership education fosters a growth mindset—the belief that abilities can be developed through effort and learning. Leaders with a growth mindset embrace challenges, persist through setbacks, learn from criticism, and find lessons in failure.

Workshops, coaching, and reflective journaling are tools often used to help leaders build this mindset. A growth-oriented leader doesn't fear failure; they see it as part of the learning process.

Ethical and Inclusive Leadership

In a diverse and interconnected world, leaders must be equipped to lead ethically and inclusively. Education plays a vital role in this preparation. Courses on ethics, equity, and cultural competence help leaders understand the impact of their decisions and create inclusive environments.

Educational programs can expose leaders to different worldviews, challenge their assumptions, and expand their understanding of fairness, justice, and responsibility.

Formal vs. Informal Learning

While universities and leadership academies provide valuable frameworks, some of the most impactful education happens informally. Real-world experiences, mistakes, feedback, and mentorship often offer deeper insights than textbooks alone.

Great leaders create a personal curriculum for themselves. They read widely, attend seminars, engage in dialogue with diverse peers, and seek mentors who stretch their thinking.

Continuous Learning and Adaptability

The most effective leaders never stop learning. They recognize that the world is evolving—and so must they. Technological advances, social change, and global interconnectivity demand adaptable leadership.

Leaders who prioritize education stay current, open-minded, and relevant. They foster a culture of learning within their teams, encouraging curiosity and development at every level.

Reflections

Education in leadership is not a destination; it is a journey. It requires humility—the acknowledgment that there is always more to learn. It demands curiosity—the drive to explore new ideas and better ways of leading. And it invites courage—the willingness to grow, even when growth is uncomfortable.

As a leader, ask yourself:

- What am I doing to continuously develop my leadership skills?
- Am I learning from my experiences, successes, and failures?
- How can I model a learning mindset for my team?

True leadership education happens in classrooms and boardrooms, in books and in conversations, in reflection and in action. The more we learn, the more we are able to serve.

Quotes

"Leadership and learning are indispensable to each other."
— John F. Kennedy

"The more that you read, the more things you will know. The more that you learn, the more places you'll go." — Dr. Seuss

---

"The illiterate of the twenty-first century will not be those who cannot read and write, but those who cannot learn, unlearn, and relearn." — Alvin Toffler

---

"An investment in knowledge always pays the best interest." — Benjamin Franklin

---

"Live as if you were to die tomorrow. Learn as if you were to live forever." — Mahatma Gandhi

---

"Education is the most powerful weapon which you can use to change the world." — Nelson Mandela

---

"Success in management requires learning as fast as the world is changing." — Warren Bennis

---

Chapter Six

Knowing When to Fold

As Chief People Officer, Edwin Brooks was responsible for leading his organization's HR strategy, talent management, and culture. However, he struggled to provide direction, accountability, and motivation. Without setting goals for himself or his team, performance declined and morale suffered.

Eventually, Edwin realized that his leadership style no longer aligned with the company's mission or his personal strengths. Rather than continuing to lead ineffectively, he made the courageous decision to step down.

By recognizing that his time in the role had reached its natural conclusion, Edwin demonstrated wisdom, self-awareness, and integrity—key traits of mature leadership. Sometimes knowing when to fold is not a sign of failure but an act of service to the organization and oneself.

The Wisdom of Letting Go

One of the most underrated qualities of a good leader is the ability to know when to walk away. Popular leadership rhetoric often focuses on perseverance, grit, and pushing through obstacles. While these traits are valuable, there are times when the best decision a leader can make is to stop, pivot, or step back entirely. Knowing when to fold isn't about giving up—it's about making space for something better.

Effective leaders are guided not only by ambition but also by discernment. They evaluate their circumstances with clarity, honesty, and objectivity. They don't allow ego, fear, or sunk costs to trap them in failing ventures or unproductive situations. Instead, they recognize when to fold—and they do so with wisdom, courage, and integrity.

Recognizing the Signs

The first step in knowing when to fold is recognizing the signs that it might be time to do so. These include:

- Persistent underperformance despite consistent effort and strategy changes.
- Toxic or unethical environments that resist change.
- Projects that no longer align with the organization's mission or values.
- Diminishing returns that no longer justify continued investment.
- Team burnout or loss of morale without a feasible path to recovery.

Leaders who are tuned into these signals are better equipped to make timely, strategic decisions.

Overcoming the Fear of Failure

One of the biggest obstacles to folding is the fear of failure. Leaders may worry that stepping away signals weakness, incompetence, or lack of commitment. In reality, walking away from something that no longer works can be the ultimate act of strength.

Letting go allows for recalibration. It creates room for innovation, new strategies, or fresh directions. Leaders who can reframe failure as feedback—and not as a personal indictment—are more agile, resilient, and ultimately more successful.

The Sunk Cost Fallacy

Leaders often stay committed to failing initiatives because of the time, energy, and money already invested. This is known as the sunk cost fallacy. It's the flawed logic that says, "We can't quit now—we've already spent so much."

Good leaders recognize that past investments should not dictate future decisions. They focus on what is best moving forward, not on what has already been lost. They understand that continuing to throw resources at a failing effort doesn't salvage the past—it endangers the future.

Strategic Abandonment

Peter Drucker, one of the most respected voices in management theory, advocated for the practice of strategic abandonment: the regular review and intentional discontinuation of activities that no longer serve a purpose. Strategic abandonment is not reactive—it's proactive. It's about making deliberate choices to stop doing things that are no longer effective, even if they once were.

This process requires discipline and clarity. Leaders must routinely evaluate:

- Are we doing this because it works, or because it's familiar?
- Does this initiative support our mission and vision?
- What would we do if we were starting fresh today?

Asking these questions ensures that resources are directed toward what matters most.

Pivoting vs. Folding

Folding doesn't always mean quitting entirely. Sometimes, it means pivoting—changing direction while preserving core goals. Great leaders know the difference. They are flexible enough to adapt without abandoning their mission.

Pivoting could mean:

- Adjusting a product or service based on customer feedback.
- Realigning team roles to better match strengths.
- Shifting target markets or strategic partnerships.

The decision to pivot or fold outright depends on whether the fundamental vision remains viable. Leaders weigh this carefully and act decisively.

Leading Through the Exit

How a leader handles the process of folding or exiting is as important as the decision itself. Transparency, empathy, and clear communication are critical. Whether closing a department, ending a project, or leaving a position, leaders must:

- Communicate the reasons clearly and respectfully.
- Acknowledge the impact on others.
- Celebrate contributions and lessons learned.
- Offer support and next steps where possible.

A graceful exit preserves relationships, protects morale, and models maturity. It shows that leadership is not just about wins—it's about responsibility.

Personal Leadership Decisions

Knowing when to fold applies not only to business strategies but to personal leadership decisions as well. This includes recognizing when:

- A leadership role no longer aligns with your values or purpose.
- Personal well-being is suffering.
- Growth and impact are limited by current constraints.

Good leaders reflect deeply and act with integrity, even when that means stepping down or transitioning to new roles. Leadership is not about clinging to position; it's about stewarding influence wisely.

The Courage to Change Course

There is courage in continuing—but also in stopping. It takes emotional maturity to admit that something is not working. It takes humility to change course. And it takes vision to see what new possibilities may emerge from letting go.

Leaders who develop this courage empower their teams to be honest, adaptable, and growth-oriented. They create cultures where reflection, flexibility, and smart risk-taking are valued more than blind perseverance.

Lessons from Nature and Business

Nature offers many lessons about knowing when to fold. Trees shed their leaves in winter to conserve energy and prepare for spring. Animals migrate when food sources dwindle. These cycles are not signs of failure—they are strategies for survival and renewal.

In business, some of the world's most successful leaders and companies have folded ventures in order to thrive. Steve Jobs left Apple, only to return and transform it. Amazon shut down its Fire Phone project, learned from it, and later launched the immensely successful Alexa. These examples show that folding can be a prelude to future success.

Trusting Your Inner Compass

Ultimately, knowing when to fold comes down to trust—trust in your intuition, your principles, and your team. The best leaders don't just rely on data and metrics; they listen to their inner compass. They ask:

- What is this situation trying to teach me?
- What future might be possible if I let go?
- What decision honors my integrity and responsibility?

When leaders trust themselves, they are free to make bold decisions that others may fear. They let go of what no longer serves and move toward what truly matters.

Reflections

Letting go is not the opposite of leadership—it is a part of it. The willingness to step away, start over, or change direction is a mark of wisdom, not weakness. It takes clarity to see the truth, courage to act on it, and grace to do so with integrity.

As a leader, consider:

- Am I holding onto something that no longer serves its purpose?
- What might I gain by letting go?
- How can I model healthy detachment and adaptability?

Growth often begins where resistance ends. Knowing when to fold is not giving up on leadership—it's leading with greater truth.

Quotes

"You got to know when to hold 'em, know when to fold 'em, know when to walk away, and know when to run." — Kenny Rogers

---

"Sometimes letting things go is an act of far greater power than defending or hanging on." — Eckhart Tolle

---

"The art of leadership is knowing when to make a move and when to move on." — John C. Maxwell

---

"Winners quit all the time. They just quit the right things at the right time." — Seth Godin

---

"Letting go means to come to the realization that some people, places, or things are a part of your history, but not a part of your destiny." — Steve Maraboli

---

Knowing When to Fold 65

"There is a time for departure even when there's no clear place to go." — Tennessee Williams

---

"True success comes not from stubbornness, but from wisdom, courage, and the grace to move on." — Unknown

Chapter Seven

A Look Into the Future of Leadership

FUTURE LEADERSHIP WILL BE SHAPED by new dynamics —embracing innovation, adapting to rapid change, fostering collaboration, supporting hybrid work, and integrating artificial intelligence responsibly.

Dallas Montgomery, CEO of a large manufacturing firm in Texas, recognized these shifts. He convened his executive team, including the Chief People Officer, to brainstorm what leadership should look like in 2035.

Together, they identified essential traits for future leaders:

- **Digital literacy** and comfort with emerging technologies
- **Critical thinking** and emotional intelligence
- **Adaptability** in a fast-changing global landscape
- **Commitment to collaboration and hybrid work**
- **Integration of AI** with accountability, transparency, and purpose

Dallas concluded the session by affirming that preparing for the future begins today—with leaders who are curious, compassionate, and committed to lifelong growth.

Embracing Change in an Uncertain World

The future of leadership is being shaped by unprecedented change. From technological breakthroughs to social revolutions, the forces that define the 21st century are demanding a new kind of leader—one who is agile, visionary, inclusive, and deeply human. Traditional hierarchies and rigid structures are giving way to more fluid, collaborative, and adaptive ways of working. In this evolving landscape, leadership is no longer about command and control; it's about cultivating environments where people thrive and innovation flourishes.

Leaders who succeed in the future will be those who embrace uncertainty, harness complexity, and lead with both heart and strategy.

The Rise of Adaptive Leadership

In a world marked by volatility and disruption, the most valuable leadership skill is adaptability. The future leader must be comfortable with ambiguity, willing to pivot quickly, and capable of leading through constant change.

Adaptive leadership is about being flexible without losing direction. It requires a mindset that views challenges as opportunities to learn and grow. Future leaders will need to build cultures that reward experimentation, value feedback, and encourage continuous learning.

They will lead not from a pedestal but from within the team, co-creating solutions and navigating uncertainty together.

Technology as a Leadership Partner

Artificial intelligence, automation, big data, and virtual collaboration tools are transforming the way we lead. Future leaders must understand these technologies—not necessarily as experts, but as strategic thinkers who can leverage their potential.

Digital fluency will be essential. Leaders will use data to make better decisions, AI to increase efficiency, and virtual platforms to build connected and high-performing teams across the globe. At the same time, they must remain vigilant about ethics, privacy, and the human impact of technological change.

The challenge will be to integrate technology in a way that enhances—not replaces—human connection and judgment.

Human-Centered and Empathetic Leadership

As machines take over routine tasks, the uniquely human aspects of leadership will become more important than ever. Empathy, emotional intelligence, and compassion will define the most effective leaders of the future.

People want to work for leaders who see them as individuals, care about their well-being, and invest in their growth. The future of leadership is deeply relational. It calls for active listening, vulnerability, and genuine connection.

Human-centered leadership also means creating inclusive workplaces where diverse voices are heard, valued, and empowered to lead.

Purpose-Driven and Ethical Leadership

Tomorrow's leaders will be held to higher standards—not just for what they accomplish, but for how they accomplish it. Employees, customers, investors, and communities expect leaders to be purpose-driven and socially responsible.

The future of leadership is anchored in values. Leaders will be expected to take a stand on issues like climate change, social justice, equity, and sustainability. They must align business goals with broader societal impact and build trust through transparency and authenticity.

This shift represents not a burden, but an opportunity—for leaders to inspire change and make meaningful contributions beyond profit.

Building Resilient and Distributed Teams

Remote work, global collaboration, and the gig economy are reshaping how teams function. Leaders of the future will lead decentralized, diverse, and dynamic teams. They will need to foster cohesion and engagement across time zones, cultures, and platforms.

This requires new skills in digital communication, cultural intelligence, and virtual team management. Future leaders will prioritize mental health, create psychologically safe environments, and use technology to connect, not divide.

They will also empower distributed leadership, recognizing that leadership is not confined to titles, but shared across the organization.

Lifelong Learning and Leadership Development

In the future, leadership is not a destination but a continuous journey. The pace of change demands that leaders remain learners. They must invest in their own development and create cultures that encourage learning at every level.

This means:

- Staying curious and open to new perspectives.
- Seeking feedback and acting on it.
- Encouraging innovation and growth within teams.

Leadership development will no longer be confined to workshops or executive training—it will be embedded in everyday experiences and available to everyone.

The New Metrics of Success

How we define success in leadership is also evolving. It's no longer just about revenue or shareholder returns. Future metrics will include:

- Employee engagement and retention.
- Impact on community and environment.
- Innovation, adaptability, and resilience.

Leaders will be evaluated on their ability to build thriving cultures, create meaningful work, and leave a positive legacy.

Reflections

Looking into the future of leadership is both exhilarating and humbling. The road ahead is filled with complexity and possibility. But one thing is clear: leadership must evolve if it is to meet the challenges of tomorrow.

The future will require leaders who are learners, connectors, listeners, and builders. Leaders who can harness technology without losing humanity. Leaders who can act with courage, clarity, and compassion.

As you prepare for this future, ask yourself:

- Am I open to growth and change?
- How am I developing others to lead?
- What kind of future do I want to help create?

The future of leadership is not something to predict. It's something to shape, together.

Quotes

> "The best way to predict the future is to create it." — Peter Drucker

A Look Into the Future of Leadership 73

"In a world that's changing really quickly, the only strategy that is guaranteed to fail is not taking risks." — Mark Zuckerberg

---

"The future belongs to those who learn more skills and combine them in creative ways." — Robert Greene

---

"Leadership is not about being in charge. It is about taking care of those in your charge." — Simon Sinek

---

"The illiterate of the future will not be those who cannot read and write, but those who cannot learn, unlearn, and relearn." — Alvin Toffler

---

"If your actions inspire others to dream more, learn more, do more and become more, you are a leader." — John Quincy Adams

---

Chapter Eight
The Golden Rule of Leadership

The Golden Rule of Leadership is simple yet profound:

"Act toward others as you would want them to act toward you."

This principle calls on leaders to lead with empathy, fairness, and respect. It promotes a culture of kindness and accountability, reminding leaders that authority should never eclipse humanity.

Former First Lady **Michelle Obama** embodies this rule. Through initiatives like *Let's Move!* and *Reach Higher*, she demonstrated how empathy and compassion can drive national impact. Her example teaches that true leadership begins not with power, but with purpose and heart.

At the heart of all great leadership lies a timeless principle: the Golden Rule. "Treat others as you would like to be treated." This rule, rooted in ancient philosophy and spiritual teachings, transcends cultures, industries, and eras.

In leadership, it is not just a moral guideline but a powerful strategic asset. It fosters trust, builds loyalty, encourages empathy, and sustains a positive and productive culture.

The Golden Rule of Leadership is about more than kindness—it's about mutual respect, dignity, and the conscious creation of environments where people feel seen, heard, and valued. Let's explore how these principals shapes extraordinary leaders and why it remains essential in the modern world.

Empathy at the Core

Empathy is the engine behind the Golden Rule. Great leaders step into the shoes of others, consider different perspectives, and seek to understand before being understood. They listen actively, respond compassionately, and treat each individual not as a means to an end but as a valuable human being.

Empathetic leadership doesn't mean always agreeing or compromising on standards—it means approaching decisions with humanity. When leaders lead with empathy, they foster loyalty, engagement, and resilience.

Trust Built on Respect

Trust is the foundation of any healthy relationship, and respect is its cornerstone. Leaders who treat others with respect—regardless of title, background, or role—create environments where people are more willing to collaborate, innovate, and speak up.

Respectful leadership is expressed through fairness, transparency, recognition, and inclusivity. It means valuing people's time, listening without interrupting, and creating space for differing viewpoints. Leaders who consistently demonstrate respect inspire the same behavior in others.

Modeling Behavior

Leadership is less about what you say and more about what you do. The Golden Rule calls for modeling the behavior you want to see in your team: integrity, accountability, humility, and grace under pressure.

When leaders act with integrity, admit mistakes, show appreciation, and offer support, they set a powerful example. Others are more likely to follow suit when they see these values practiced, not just preached.

This modeling extends to tone, energy, and even body language. A leader's presence can either elevate or diminish the collective morale of a team.

Feedback with Compassion

Feedback is one of the most effective tools for growth. But how it is delivered matters as much as what is said. Leaders guided by the Golden Rule deliver feedback in the way they would like to receive it: respectfully, constructively, and with care.

They balance candor with compassion, and they separate behavior from identity. They praise in public and correct in private. In doing so, they foster a culture where feedback is not feared but welcomed.

Navigating Conflict Fairly

Conflict is inevitable in leadership, but how leaders handle it defines the outcome. The Golden Rule encourages leaders to approach conflict with fairness and empathy. Instead of assigning blame, they seek understanding. Instead of escalating tension, they focus on resolution.

Leaders who apply the Golden Rule in conflict recognize the dignity of all parties. They practice patience, prioritize communication, and strive for solutions that respect everyone involved.

Empowerment Through Trust

Treating others as you wish to be treated also means trusting them as you wish to be trusted. Great leaders delegate responsibility, encourage autonomy, and give others room to shine. They don't micromanage—they empower.

Empowered teams are more creative, accountable, and invested in their work. Leaders who trust their people foster a culture of ownership and initiative.

Long-Term Impact

The effects of the Golden Rule are not always immediate, but they are lasting. Teams led by compassionate, ethical, and fair leaders tend to be more loyal, more resilient, and more successful over time. People remember how they were treated more than what goals were achieved.

The Golden Rule contributes to sustainable leadership. It builds reputations, strengthens relationships, and attracts talent. In a fast-changing world, the leaders who consistently treat others well will stand out and endure.

Reflections

The Golden Rule is simple, but not always easy. It requires self-awareness, discipline, and emotional intelligence. In moments of stress, competition, or conflict, it's tempting to act from fear or ego. But the leaders who return to this principle—even under pressure—build cultures of excellence and character.

As a leader, ask yourself:

- Am I treating my team with the same respect I expect?
- Do my actions reflect the leadership values I admire in others?
- How can I model the Golden Rule in difficult situations?

Leadership is not about power—it's about service. The Golden Rule reminds us that leadership, at its best, is profoundly human.

Quotes

> "People will forget what you said, people will forget what you did, but people will never forget how you made them feel." — Maya Angelou

"Do to others whatever you would like them to do to you. This is the essence of all that is taught." — Matthew 7:12

"Leadership is not about being in charge. It's about taking care of those in your charge." — Simon Sinek

---

"The way you treat people is the way you invite them to treat you." — Unknown

---

"Respect is how to treat everyone, not just those you want to impress." — Richard Branson

---

"Kindness is a language that the deaf can hear and the blind can see." — Mark Twain

Author's Note: Why I Wrote This Book

This book was born out of a deep concern and a personal calling. Over the course of my career, I have witnessed many individuals in leadership and management roles who were neither prepared for the responsibilities nor motivated by the right reasons. Too often, people pursue leadership for personal gain, status, or control—rather than from a genuine desire to lead with integrity, empathy, and vision.

Furthermore, I've seen too many people in leadership positions who simply shouldn't be there. Some didn't have the skills. Others didn't care about the people they were supposed to lead. They were in it for the title, the paycheck, the power—anything but the actual responsibility of leading. And when that happens, everyone under them suffers.

As a professional Human Resources leader within an elite government agency, I witnessed the best and worst of leadership. I saw inspiring examples of integrity, fairness, and courage—but I also encountered poor leadership, marked by bias, insecurity, and fear of accountability.

Throughout my career, I experienced firsthand the challenges that women—especially women of color—face in the workplace. We were often treated differently from some of our counterparts, not because of our abilities, but because of perceptions and prejudices beyond our control.

One experience stands out vividly. I once worked under a supervisor who, I believe, simply did not like me. One of my tasks was to prepare panel minutes—something I did thoroughly and professionally. Yet, no matter how carefully I wrote them, she always found fault. She frequently praised one male colleague as "the best writer in the division," so one day, I decided to test that belief. I asked him to draft the minutes for me. When I turned them in under my name, she returned them covered in her usual red circles. That's when I realized the issue had little to do with my writing and everything to do with me.

I later told her who had actually written the minutes. She was speechless—and years later, she apologized. By then, it was too late. The damage had already been done, though the lesson remained clear: leadership without fairness is not leadership at all.

That same supervisor once told me I should take voice lessons because my voice was too deep. I remember thinking, *this is the voice God gave me—and I am not about to change it.* Leaders must learn to accept others for who they are, not who they wish them to be.

I have also witnessed managers who avoided the difficult parts of leadership—those who would write annual performance appraisals without ever speaking to their employees about performance during the year. The first time those employees heard negative feedback was when they read it on paper. By then, it was too late for meaningful improvement. If you cannot have honest conversations because you fear confrontation, management may not be your calling. Leadership requires courage—the courage to do what's right, not what's easy.

I've seen promotions handed to individuals who were unqualified, simply because they interviewed well or said all the right things. But once in the job, they were unable to perform. This happens far too often—in both the workplace and, sadly, even in the church.

These and many other experiences inspired me to write this book on leadership. My hope is that by sharing what I have witnessed—the triumphs and the failures—future leaders will reflect, learn, and commit to leading with heart, fairness, and purpose.

About the Author

Gwendolyn Nadean Mathews is a seasoned leader and human resources professional with a distinguished career spanning decades in both local government and federal service. Originally from Pittsburgh, Pennsylvania, she began her leadership journey as the Director of Personnel for Community Action Pittsburgh—before the field transitioned to what is now known as Human Resources. Her early work laid a strong foundation for a lifetime commitment to people-focused leadership.

Gwendolyn holds a master's degree in Personnel and Human Resources from American University. In 1980, she relocated to Northern Virginia and began a long tenure with the Federal Government. There, she served as a Personnel and Human Resources Officer, becoming a respected manager and mentor during her fifteen 15 years in leadership prior to retirement.

Even in retirement, her passion for the field remains strong. She continues to serve as a contractor in the Human Resources sector, offering her expertise and experience to organizations in need of seasoned guidance. A lifelong learner and teacher, Gwendolyn has always aspired to write a book on leadership and management—driven by a desire to share real-world wisdom with those navigating the challenges of leadership today.

Her leadership style—firm, fair, and rooted in deep respect—has earned her lasting admiration from colleagues and team members alike. Through this book, she offers the lessons, stories, and principles that shaped her journey, with the hope of inspiring the next generation of leaders to lead with clarity, courage, and compassion.

.

www.ingramcontent.com/pod-product-compliance
Lightning Source LLC
LaVergne TN
LVHW050024080526
838202LV00069B/6910